Millennium

English

READER V

Text
Indira Srinivasan
Parvathi Krishnan

Illustrations
Dinesh Desai

BPI EDUCATIONAL

BPI EDUCATIONAL is an imprint of
BPI (INDIA) PVT LTD

ISBN 81-7693-041-5

Published by

BPI EDUCATIONAL
229/A 2nd Floor Krantiveer Rajguru Marg Girgaon
Mumbai 400 004 Tel 380 8817 / 19 e-mail bpipl@vsnl.com

CHENNAI
No 1 Second Street Nandanam Extension Chennai 600 035
Tel 433 1953 / 436 3417 e-mail quartett@md3.vsnl.net.in

PUNE
7 & 8 Shree Vidya Apartments Third Floor 116 Budhwar Peth
Pune 411 002 Tel 448 1289 / 448 7271 e-mail qbdpune@vsnl.com

Publisher's Note

The Millennium English series comprises Readers, Workbooks and Teachers' Manuals. There are two introductory books, OA and OB, for pre-primary classes and 5 Readers and Workbooks for classes 1 to 5, which constitute the complete primary language development package. The books reflect current thinking about language learning and syllabus design and also introduce learning strategies to promote learner autonomy.

The Readers are the core books of the series. This Reader focuses on:

- texts, mostly in story format, based on cross-curricular and cross-cultural themes;
- a variety of questions and activities to motivate and create the necessary environment for learning the language;
- developing the four basic language skills of listening, speaking, reading and writing;
- enriching vocabulary through intensive practise with words in the text and word extension exercises;
- enabling activities which lead to focussed and appropriate writing;
- recycling language from the earlier units to aid retention of language;
- fun elements for a positive reinforcement of the material;
- sensitizing the learner to the subtler and finer nuances of life and language through poems;
- developing through the text matter, positive values and attitudes like kindness to animals, preservation of the environment, caring for others, helping one another and respect for the living.

The format

This book has 8 units. Six of them have a poem, each of which is linked thematically to the reading text in the unit. An attempt has been made to sensitize learners to the finer nuances of language through the poems. They are introduced to some simple poetic devices like rhyme, rhythm, similes, alliteration and metaphors.

The reading texts have seven distinctive sections:

- Think (stimulates learning)
- Help to Understand (develops reading skills)
- Useful Words (enriches and extends vocabulary)
- Language in Use (from class 4 – serves as a framework for usage in language structure)
- Before You Write (helps with the process of writing)
- Now Write (provides for appropriate writing)
- Game Time (helps consolidate learning)

The Teachers' Manual provides step by step back up for the Reader. Model question papers for effective evaluation of the skills learnt have been provided in the Teachers' Manual.

Suggestions to the teacher:

- Read the Teachers' Manual before you start the course.
- Make lesson planning an integral part of your teaching.
- Make full use of the help provided in the Manual to ensure that both you and your students derive the maximum benefit from Millennium English Reader 5.

It is sincerely hoped that this course will make teaching and learning of language an enjoyable, fun experience and help equip the learner with the success skills required to meet the demands and challenges of present day academics.

Contents

1 A PLACE FOR EVERYTHING

Think : A

Do you quarrel with your friend?
What is it usually about?

Read

The Mountain and the Squirrel

The mountain and the squirrel
Had a quarrel.
And the former called the latter
"Little Prig".
Bun replied "You are doubtless very big,
But all sorts of things and weather
Must be taken in together,
To make up a year
And a sphere.

And I think it no disgrace
To occupy my place.
If I'm not so large as you,
You are not so small as I,
And not half so spry!
I'll not deny, you make
A very pretty squirrel track.
Talents differ; all is well and wisely put;
If I cannot carry forests on my back,
Neither can you crack a nut."

R.W. Emerson

Help to Understand

a. Answer the following questions:

1. Who had a quarrel?
2. Why did they quarrel?
3. Why did the squirrel say "I think it ..... occupy my place."?
4. How do you know that the mountain is very strong?
5. What could the squirrel do that the mountain couldn't do?

b. Find the words from the poem that rhyme with the following words:

prig ________	disgrace ________
weather ________	I ________
year ________	track ________

c. Work in pairs. Make up four pairs of rhyming words.

Write a short poem using these rhyming words.

Think : B

"Every home should have a pet animal."

Do you agree with this statement?

In groups of three discuss the above statement, giving reasons for your opinion.

Your teacher will ask you to share your feelings with the rest of the class.

Remember to respect each other's ideas.

Read

For the Love of a Cat

Long ago, in Japan there lived a young painter. He was a good painter and was happiest when he was deep in his work, drawing or painting. His only friend was a little cat, who shared his hut and his food and who sat quietly by him whilst he worked. It wasn't easy, though, for him to make a living. So most of the time he was poor.

One winter, life was very hard. No one gave him work, and no one in his small town could or would buy the paintings he made. At last all his paper and paints were finished and he had money left for just one more meal.

Out he went to the bazaar and brought back a small fish. "This may be the last meal of my life," he said to himself, "so I shall cook it very carefully and enjoy it. Then I'll lie down and wait for death to come."

So he prepared the fish as skillfully as he knew how and then sat down before his steaming plate. Just as he was about to take the first mouthful he suddenly saw his cat. The little creature was looking up at him with hunger in her eyes.

The painter paused. He smiled at his cat, and stroked it. "You eat the fish. I won't be able to give you anything more." So the cat ate up the fish and the young painter lay down to die.

He had hardly closed his eyes when there was a sharp knocking at the door of his hut. "Come in," he said weakly. He had no idea who it could be but he didn't care, for he had nothing that could be stolen. The painter opened his eyes and saw four priests from the largest temple in the area. "We want a large and most beautiful painting of the Holy One with all the creatures of nature around him. Name your price. We will pay you generously," they said.

In no time, an advance was paid to the young man. He and his cat ate well and then he purchased all the materials he needed. He moved into the temple and began the great work. There was only one instruction from the priests. "You may paint whatever you like. But the creature you must not include in your painting, is a cat. There must be no cats as the Holy One did not like them."

It was a small condition, so the painter accepted it and with great joy began to work. For weeks he worked quietly, speaking to no one except occasionally to his small friend and companion. He painted all the creatures. After some days he realised that his little cat was very weak and dying. "Oh, my dear little friend, what is wrong with you? Why do you lie so sadly, looking only at my painting and refusing to eat?"

He stroked her lovingly and for the first time since he began the painting, thought deeply about her. At last he looked up.

"Ah, I know what's troubling you! You are not in the painting. I'm sorry, but you know what the priests' condition was." Still, he went on looking at the troubled creature. "How can I leave you out of the world of the Holy One? You, my little loving friend, shall be there. But don't mind if I draw you small. No one will see where you are. Only you and I will know that you are there." So he painted the little cat with great care at the feet of the Buddha. When it was finished, the painter stroked his friend. She was so weak, he knew he had discovered her trouble too late to save her.

"See," he said softly, "you too are with the Holy One."

The cat looked at him with gratitude and died peacefully in his arms.

(A folk tale from Japan)

Retold by **C.Byrde**

Help to Understand

a. On the basis of your reading complete the following:

1. Drawing and painting gave the young painter ______________________________
____
____

2. He was very poor because ______________________________
____
____

3. The painter did not eat the fish because ______________

4. He was not bothered by the knocking on his door because

____

____

5. The priests had come to ______________

____

6. The one condition laid down by them was ______________

____

7. As the painter worked he did not notice ______________

____

8. The cat was sad because ______________

____

9. The painter decided ______________

____

10. The cat died peacefully because ______________

____

b. The story does not end there. In pairs, think of an answer for the following question: what do you think happened when the priests saw the painting?
(The original ending is on page 110)

c. Work in pairs A and B. A is the painter, B is the head priest. B will frame three questions. Example: What was the condition we laid down? A will answer the questions.

Useful Words

a. Match the following verbs and adverbs as used in the passage:

verbs	adverbs
pay	quietly
cook	weakly
speak	skillfully
said	generously
sat	occasionally
prepared	carefully

b. Look at the following expressions:

- deep in his work
- to make a living

What do they mean? Such expressions are called idioms. The meanings are usually not clear or obvious but the context helps us to understand them. So we know that 'deep in his work' means 'fully involved / interested in his work' and 'make a living' means 'earn a livelihood'.

What do you think the following idioms mean?

1. life was hard
2. troubled creature

Complete the following idioms:

☞ has a heart of ____________________

☞ as hard as ____________________

☞ as slow as a ____________________

☞ as fit as a ____________________

Language in Use

The town people are discussing the incident. They are angry with the painter for having disobeyed the priest. However, a few of them symphathise with him.

Read the following dialogue:

Citizen A : I think it was very wicked of him (the painter) to disobey the instructions.

Citizen B : I agree with you. He went against orders.

Citizen C : I don't think we should judge him harshly.

Citizen D : Yes, I see no reason for punishing him.

In groups of four A, B, C, D continue the dialogue. The following expressions may prove useful.

I quite agree

I'm against the idea

I see no objection

I object to ....

I favour ....

I disagree with.

Before You Write

You and a group of friends have decided to form an association called "Friends of Animals.'

In groups of four discuss how you would help animals.

Consider pet animals as well as stray animals.

Think of food, shelter, care of sick and weak animals.

Now Write

Prepare a pamphlet to be distributed in the neighbourhood. Write ten sentences.

Example : Avoid throwing stones at animals.

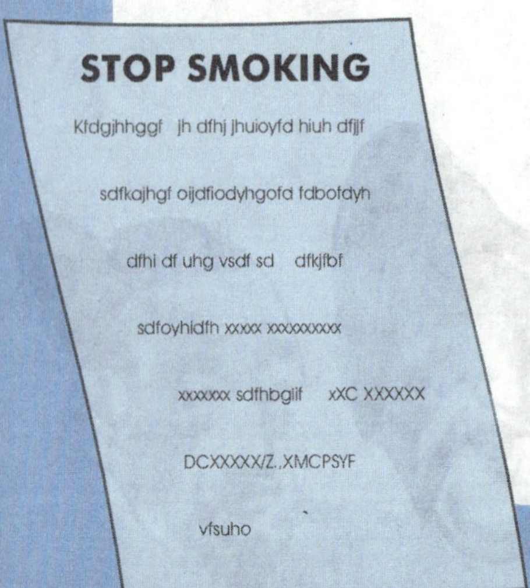

Give your pamphlet a heading.

Example : Kindness does not hurt.

Write short, clear sentences.

Game Time

Tongue Twisters

Swan swam over the pond. Swim swan swim. Swan swam back again. Well swum swan.

Your teacher will help you read the tongue twister correctly first. Then get into groups of 4. Practise in your group. Prepare one person in your group to recite well. Your teacher will then ask the group representatives to recite. The one who recites quickly thrice without making any mistakes is from the winning group.

Collect more tongue twisters. Example: She sells seashells on the sea shore.

2 ENVIRONMENT

Think : A

Work with a partner. List a few things you enjoy doing in a garden.

List a few things you don't like about gardening.

Read

A Girl's Garden

A neighbour of mine in the village,
Likes to tell how one spring,
When she was a girl on the farm, she did
A child-like thing.

One day she asked her father,
To give her a garden plot
To plant and tend and reap herself,
And he said, "Why not?'

In casting* about for a corner,
He thought of an idle bit
Of walled-off ground, where a shop had stood,
And he said, "Just it."

And he said, "That ought to make you
An ideal one-girl farm,
And give you a chance to put some strength
On your slim-jim arm."

It was not enough of a garden
Her father said, to plough;
So she had to work it all by hand,
But she don't mind it now.

She wheeled the dung in the wheelbarrow,
Along a stretch of road;
But she always ran away and left
Her not-nice load

And hid from anyone passing,
And then she begged the seed.
She says she thinks she planted one
Of all things but weed.*

A hill each of potatoes,
Radishes, Lettuce, Peas,
Tomatoes, Beets, Beans, Pumpkins, Corn
And even fruit trees.

And yes, she has long mistrusted
That a Cider Apple tree
In bearing there today is hers,
Or at least may be.

– **Robert Frost**

(*casting = looking about,
weed = wild plant)

Help to Understand

a. Answer the following questions:

1. What was the 'child-like thing' the neighbour did?
2. What did she want to do with the 'garden plot'?
3. Why did her father call it a one-girl farm?
4. Her father felt that work on the farm would change her. How?
5. Why did she leave the wheelbarrow on the road?
6. Why did she 'beg' the seed?
7. Did she really grow all the things mentioned on her farm? Pick out a line from stanza 7 in support of your answer.
8. Do you think she had planted a Cider Apple seed? Why/Why not?

b. The poet uses a number of compound words (i.e) two words written with a hyphen:

They are walled-off (ground)
one-girl (farm)
slim-jim (arm)
not-nice (load)

c. Make suitable compound words with the following sets of words.
Match them from the two boxes A and B:

A	B
curly, broken, long, left, tight	handed, legged, down, fitting, haired

d. Use the compound words to fill in the blanks in the following sentences:

1. The ____________ child had a beautiful red bow on her head.

2. The ____________ teenager came first in the race.

3. The bowlers found it difficult to get the ____________ batsman out.

4. A crane had to tow away the ____________ bus.

5. The man in the ____________ jeans was the last to leave the room.

e. Pick out the words associated with farming.

Example: plants, ____________

f. What do you associate with the following sets of words? Choose the words from the box below:

1. sweet, bitter, salty, spicy, sour ____________

2. boil, fry, bake, roast, grill ____________

3. lawyer, dentist, architect, accountant, engineer ____________

4. cold, warm, chilly, humid, damp ____________

5. silk, cotton, velvet, leather, denim ____________

weather, taste, working, clothes, profession

Think : B

1. Close your eyes and imagine a world without trees. What would it look like? Complete the following sentence:

   A world without trees would ______________________________

2. Work with a partner and add five more words to the ones given below.

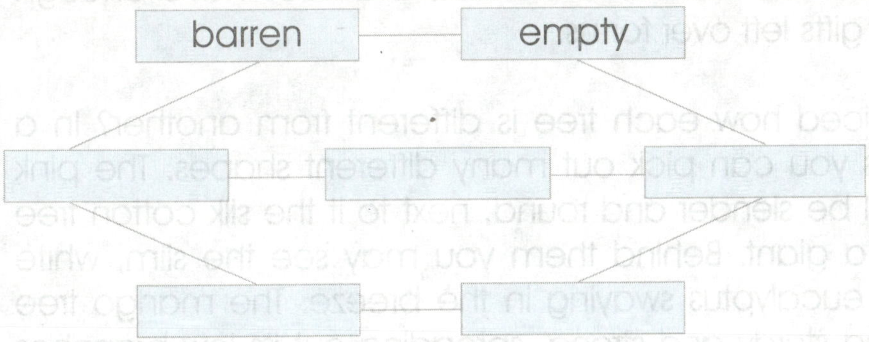

Read

Trees

Look up at any large tree. Can you see a pair of small eyes staring back at you? It could be a squirrel clinging to the tree trunk or a colony of bats swinging from the branches. Trees shelter all kinds of birds, animals and insects. Every part of the tree from the roots to the canopy is home to some small creature.

Trees not only allow their tenants to live rent-free but feed them too. Buds, flowers, fruits and leaves of many shapes and colours are offered as food by the generous trees. And after taking care of the needs of small creatures, the trees have enough gifts left over for us.

Have you noticed how each tree is different from another? In a group of trees you can pick out many different shapes. The pink cassia tree will be slender and round, next to it the silk cotton tree will tower like a giant. Behind them you may see the slim, white trunk of a tall eucalyptus swaying in the breeze. The mango tree will be standing sturdy and strong, spreading out its low branches that make it such a good tree to climb. The banyan tree has dense foliage – a good, shady place to build a secure bee-hive. The eagle wants a nest from which it can scan its surroundings, so it picks a high airy tree like the silver oak. Some trees have a smooth bark which feels like paper when you touch it, while others have rough, furrowed barks which the insects like to explore.

Can you imagine what would happen to all the small animals and birds if there were no trees to shelter and feed them? These little creatures repay the tree's kindness by helping to spread the seeds. We too should realize how important trees are to us and when a new tree grows from the seed, we must make sure it is allowed to become another large, generous tree.

Help to Understand

On the basis of your reading answer the following:

1. Write the names of three creatures that live on trees.
2. What four things do trees offer as food to these creatures?
3. Mention two things that are different from one tree to another.
4. What do birds and animals do to help trees?
5. Write down the names of the trees mentioned in the text.
6. How should we help trees?

Useful Words

a. In column A, there are some words which describe trees. Match them with their meanings in column B.

A	B
1. slender	strong
2. smooth	find out something
3. dense	persons who live in a rented house.
4. furrowed	not rough
5. explore	closely packed
6. sturdy	thin
7. tenants	uneven

A compound adjective is an adjective which is made up of two parts and is usually written with a hyphen. For example, bell-shaped, five-petaled, cherry-sized. Its meaning is usually clear from the words it combines.

Fill each of the blanks to form a new compound adjective.
Use a dictionary if necessary.

1. ______________ eyed
2. ______________ minded
3. ______________ heeled
4. ______________ hearted
5. ______________ tailed
6. ______________ sighted

Language in Use

Amit and Jaya are talking about growing more trees.

Read the following dialogue.

Let's do something to grow more trees.

Why don't we buy some saplings?

That's a good idea! Where shall we plant them?

Let us ask our friends to plant a tree in each house.

When we discuss ideas the following expressions are useful:

How about ....

Perhaps, we should...

I feel .....

Could we ....

I'm not so sure ....

I'm afraid that's not possible but ....

Think of similar situations where these expressions could be used. Follow the example.

Before You Write

Form groups of three, A, B, C. Discuss what should be done to save the trees. Use the expressions from the previous exercise while discussing.

A will speak about the usefulness of trees.

B will speak about how we can help to grow more trees.

C will speak about what will happen if we have no trees.

Write down the points.

Now Write

After the discussion write an essay on why we should protect trees and grow more trees. Consult each other for ideas exchange your work. Suggest corrections and improvements. You may find the following format useful.

Introduction : Trees – their usefulness to us.

Body : Ways in which trees are useful

1. provide shelter and shade
2. retain moisture
3. protect the environment

Conclusion : Ways of growing more trees

Game Time

Leaf-Prints

You need:

- green leaves and ferns of different shapes and sizes.
- thick poster paints
- a plate or tray
- sheets of paper
- a paint brush

How to take prints:

- Spread some thick poster paint on a tray. Lay a leaf on it and press it down gently to coat one side with paint.
- Pick up the leaf and put it, painted side down on a sheet of paper. Cover it with another sheet of paper and rub it gently all over with the side of your hand.
- Pick up the top sheet and lift off the leaf gently, without smudging the paint.
- On a big sheet of paper, take many leaf prints to make an unusual wrapping paper.

2. In pairs, think and note down as many things as you can that fit into a matchbox. The items will have to be small enough to fit into a matchbox. The pair that can think of the most items is the winner.

Variations to the game can be:

How many things can you think of that ....

1. are long and thin?

2. work on electricity?

3. make a noise?

3 RAMAN CATCHES A THIEF

Think

In pairs discuss what you would do :

1. if you came across a stray dog in your neighbourhood park.
2. if you noticed a big spider crawling up your leg during assembly in school.

Your teacher will ask you for your ideas.

Read

Tenali Raman and a Thief

It was a chilly dark night. Tenali Raman returned home tired and hungry after a hard day's work in the fields. His wife had kept dinner ready for him. He ate it and went to the backyard to wash his hands. His wife fetched water for him in a brass pot.

He was about to wash his hands when he saw somebody hiding behind a pile of firewood. Raman knew it was a thief; he was waiting there for the family to go to sleep. Then he could enter the house and steal everything. Raman's wife did not see the thief. Raman kept quiet because he did not want to frighten her. He thought for a moment and emptied the pot of water on the thief. But the thief did not get up. He was afraid he would be caught if he moved. So he remained still in his hiding place.

Raman shouted for some water in a bigger pot. His wife asked herself, "What is he up to now? He wants more water and in a bigger pot now!" However she fetched it and gave it to him. Then she went in to attend to her work.

Within a few minutes she again heard Raman crying out, "I want some more water in a still bigger vessel." She was amazed at this and was curious to know what he did with all the water. So she filled a huge vessel and carried it to Raman with great difficulty. Then she stood behind the door and watched him. She was surprised to see him empty the water on the pile of firewood!

She came out and shouted at Raman, "What are you doing? Why did you pour all the water on the firewood? It will be damp and how can I light it in the kitchen?" Raman did not reply, but made her fetch water again and again.

During all this time the thief did not utter a sound. He sat quietly, wet and shivering in the cold!

Raman's wife patiently went on bringing water wondering at the strange behaviour of her husband! She became very tired when she fetched water for the tenth time. Her temper and strength ran out and she yelled at him, "Have you gone crazy? How many times am I to bring water for you? And you still have not washed your hands. Why are you behaving like this?" Raman took the pot from her, without answering or looking at her.

He was about to throw the water on the thief, when his wife shouted at him, "I am talking to you. Don't waste one drop of water. I will not bring you anymore."

Raman stood still with the potful of water, glaring at his wife. He could see that she was very tired and angry. Yet he said, "Stop shouting and behave yourself. I told you not to question me."

His wife straightened herself and cried angrily, "I will not be shouted at. I am not your slave. My back is broken and my feet are aching."

"How dare you talk to me like this?" shouted back Raman, his temper rising.

"Who cares?" screamed Raman's wife. "I am not afraid of you. I am going to sleep now. You can spend the rest of the night fetching hundred potfuls of water and throwing it on the firewood."

So saying she was about to turn back, when Raman in great anger, emptied all the water on her head. Stunned, she let out a piercing scream, that brought all the neighbours to Raman's courtyard.

Now the neighbours had heard the noise from Raman's house for quite some time. They were disturbed from their sleep and were annoyed. So they all came to Raman's house in a great fury. But they were surprised to find Raman's wife wet from head to foot at this time of the night! She was stamping her feet and weeping.

"What's happening here Raman, at this late hour?" they asked anxiously. "Why is your wife crying like this? And she is so wet too. Tell us. We want some peace and quiet."

Raman took a deep breath and answered slowly. "My friends, do not be angry with me. I will explain everything. Just be patient. You all know how fond I am of my wife."

"That is why we are surprised at what you have done to her," said one of the neighbours angrily.

Raman continued, "I married her when she was very young. Since then I have fed her, clothed her and attended to all her needs. I have built this nice house for her. I made her happy when she was sad. I looked after her when she was ill and nursed her back to health. And now she has turned against me because I threw one potful of water on her head!

On the other hand can you believe that an utter stranger to whom I have not done anything sits quietly when I pour several pots of cold water on his head? Can you believe it?" he asked again.

The crowd murmured, "How can we believe it? No one will sit quietly if you pour cold water on his head in this weather."

Raman said, "If you don't believe me, ask the person sitting behind the firewood pile."

At this point the thief knowing his game was up, gave a jump and tried to run away. Immediately the crowd chased him shouting, "Thief! Thief!" and caught him.

Then one of them turned to Raman and said with a smile, "Raman you are a very clever man. Your wife is indeed lucky. You found out a way to catch the thief with our help. Otherwise you would have been alone and he might have attacked you in this dark night." All the others nodded their heads in agreement and marched off with the thief to the jail.

Raman then addressed his wife who had become speechless by now, "Come let us go in. You will catch a cold. You must dry yourself and wear another saree."

Raman's wife looked at her husband for a moment and burst into peals of laughter which could be heard all over. Raman joined her in this and they both went inside the house.

– **Kamala Laxman**

Help to Understand

a. Given below is a summary of the story but there are some incorrect statements. Find them and correct them.

Raman of Tenali noticed a thief in his backyard when he went to wash his hands after dinner. He poured the water on the thief, who kept quiet. So Raman called his wife and told her about the thief. Then he asked her to bring smaller pots of water which he poured on the thief who was hiding behind the trees and who kept quiet all the while. Raman's wife was quite annoyed by then and refused to bring any more water. This angered Raman and he threw the water on her. She began screaming. This brought all the neighbours to their yard. The neighbours asked Raman to explain things. He said that his wife had gone mad. He narrated how he had looked after her all his life but she had turned against him when he threw a pot of water on her. On the other hand, an utter stranger had kept quiet while he had been pouring pots of water on him.

The thief knew the game was up. He was caught by the crowd when he tried to run away. Everyone congratulated Raman on his clever plan.

b. Answer the following questions briefly:

1. "He wants more water and in a bigger pot too."
   Who said these words and to whom? Who is 'he'?

2. "Stop shouting and behave yourself!" Who said these words? To whom, and why?

3. "What's happening here, at this late hour? We want some peace and quiet." Who said these words, to whom and why?

4. "Come let us go in. You will catch a cold. You must dry yourself." Who said these words, to whom? Why was the person likely to catch a cold?

Useful Words

a. Make word partnerships with the following sets of words. Example: dark night

Note: They have been used in the story.

A	B
strange	difficulty
piercing	breath
deep	behaviour
great	scream
hiding	place

b. Use these word pairs in the following sentences:

1. When the little girl saw the tiger she let out a ____________

2. The swimming champion took a ____________ before he dived into the pool.

3. The parents were puzzled by their son's ____________

4. The squirrel stored the nuts in a secret ____________

5. All the shops were closed during the strike. It was with ____________ ____________ that he managed to buy the medicines.

Language in Use

Look at the sentences below. Which of these is a more polite expression?

1. "I want some water in a bigger vessel"

2. "Could I have some more water in a bigger vessel? "

Rewrite the following in a more polite way:

1. What are you doing? – Could you ____________________
2. You will do as I tell you – Please ____________________
3. We want some peace and quiet – Could we ____________________
4. Shut the door – Could ____________________
5. I want a box of chocolates – ____________________

Before You Write

In groups of three read the following account. Discuss the incident and jot down the points:

Students of class V-A have been losing a number of cycle parts from the school, for example : bells, seat covers, locks, tubes, lights. Although a number of complaints have been made to the watchman, no action has been taken so far.

The students decide to form a committee, to keep a close watch and to find the culprit. As they need permission to do this, they decide to write to the Principal about the thefts and to seek permission for the suggested action.

While discussing ...

First, draw up a list of items lost and when they were lost.

Secondly, a possible list of suspects.

Thirdly, action to be taken – a watch squad to be formed.

Finally, permission to put the plan into action.

Read out your points to the rest of the class.

Now Write

Write the letter to the Principal using the following format:

Students of Class V-A

__________________ School.

Nagpur

Date

The Principal

__________________ School

Nagpur

Dear Sir / Madam,

We, the students of Class V-A, wish to bring to your notice

____

____

Yours faithfully

(Students of Class V—A)

Game Time

Two students stand with their backs to the board. They are 'detectives'. The teacher will write a brief situation.

Example: the school is on fire.
The rest of the class are witnesses and suggest evidence – sight, smell, sounds.

Example:
I can smell smoke.
It's getting hotter.
People are jumping out of the window.
I can hear the alarm bell.

The detectives have to guess the situation from the evidence.

4 GET SET GO

Think : A

There are different modes of transport. You can travel from one place to another, by road, by air, by river/sea or by rail.

Work with a partner and fill in the following table. Mention one advantage and one disadvantage of each mode.

mode	advantage	disadvantage
1. by road		
2. by rail		
3. by sea		
4. by air		

Read

The World from a Railway Carriage

Faster than fairies, faster than witches,
Bridges and houses, hedges and ditches,
And charging along like troops in a battle,
All through the meadows, the horses and cattle.

All of the sights of the hill and the plain,
Fly as thick as driving rain;
And ever again in the wink of an eye,
Painted stations whistle by.

Here is a child who clambers and scrambles,
All by himself and gathering brambles;
Here is a tramp who stands and gazes;
And there is the green for stringing the daisies!

Here is a cart run away in the road,
Lumping along with man and load;
And here is a mill and there is a river;
Each a glimpse and gone for ever.

– **R. L. Stevenson**

(scrambles: to move quickly, gazes: to look at something for long, brambles: the wild black berry bush, glimpse: a quick look at something, tramp: a person with no home or job)

Help to Understand

1. Make a list of the things you can see from a railway carriage.
2. Pick out words that describe movement.
   Example: faster

3. Why do the 'horses and cattle' appear to be "charging along like troops ...." ?

4. The poet mentions many natural sights and animals. Who are the people he describes?

5. Does the train stop anywhere in this poem?

6. Why does the poet call the sights "a glimpse and gone for ever"?

7. The following words describe the movement of the train:

   charging, flying, running by

   Place them in their ascending order of speed.
   Example : fast, faster, fastest

8. Arrange the following verbs on a similar scale, from slow to fastest :

   run, crawl, walk, amble, trot, plod, streak.

Think : B

Read the following items:

A young petite girl Usha Gowri who had an ambition to become a doctor, to serve suffering humanity set an example when she donated her kidneys to two needy persons after her death - *The Hindu, YoungWorld*

Disha, a young farm worker suffered third degree burns when she rescuedher mother and little brother from a fire in their hut ..... *Indian Express*

Fourteen year old Raju battled the currentsof a river in flood to save his six year old neighbour Jagan .... *Deccan Chronicle*

What adjectives would you use to describe the three persons mentioned here? Example: brave,......

Compare them with your partner's list.

Read

Work in pairs A and B. All the As read passage A. All the Bs read passage B.

Passage A :

Dinko : The Golden Boy

Twenty year old Dinko was born in Sekta village which is about 20 km. from Imphal, Manipur. His father was a poor farmer living a miserable existence in difficult conditions.

Unable to bear the burden of poverty, Dinko's father died when Dinko was quite young. Dinko hardly remembered his father. His mother was left all alone to bring up eight children – four sons and four daughters. With no one to help her or guide her, she left home and went to live elsewhere. Her elder sons died of malnutrition while Dinko went to live in an orphanage called Children's Home. It was a difficult existence but there were boys of his age group. They had frugal meals – mostly rice, dal, and a little curry. Dinko and his friend Surjit spent a great deal of their time practising boxing, judo and kungfu. In fact, it kept him alive in spite of the "hunger in his belly", says Dinko.

Hard work brought recognition. When Dinko was about thirteen years old, he was spotted by a boxing coach Ibonicha who recognised his skills as those belonging to a future champion. From then onwards, there was no rest. Determination and a desire to excel helped Dinko overcome hunger and fatigue. He worked hard with his coach. Five years later he got recognition in the National Games but it was the '98 Asiad at Bangkok which brought him the much-acclaimed gold medal. It was a proud moment for both India and Dinko as he had won a gold in boxing for his nation.

People of Sekta, his hometown, rejoiced all night. They sang and danced. His sister Rani and coach Ibonicha were congratulated by everyone.

The story of Dinko is an inspiration to all those who wish to achieve their ambitions. Overcoming hunger and poverty, he worked hard to reach his goal. The whole nation is proud of this humble boy who achieved the distinction of winning a gold medal at the Asiad.

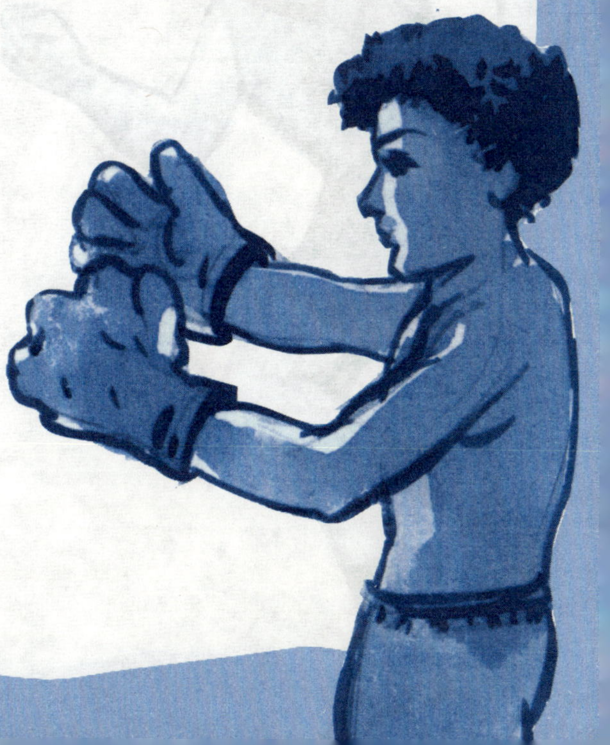

Passage : B

Jyotirmoyee : India's New Golden Girl

Born in Debogram village in West Bengal's Nadia district, Jyotirmoyee Sikdar was the fifth child of a struggling couple, Gurudas Sikdar and his wife Nehar. Her father was a retired pole vaulter.

The children had little to eat, not even a glass of milk. But Jyotirmoyee did not complain. She shared whatever she had with her brothers and sisters. Her mother was worried about this frail and weak child and did not encourage her love of athletics. But Jyotirmoyee practised running through the fields and nursed her ambition of becoming an athlete. When she won all the five athletic events in her Annual School Sports meet she was afraid to show the medals to her mother. She confided in her father. Recognising her talent, he encouraged her to practise her skills. Her first coach, Satya Ranjan Roy spent hours teaching her the basic skills. Years of hard work were rewarded when she won recognition in the National Games and then at the Asiad'94 where she came fourth. But it was her golden hour at Bangkok in 1998 when she won the golds for the 1500m and the 800m events respectively. Twenty nine year old Jyotirmoyee had realised her ambition. On the day of the 1500m race Jyotirmoyee was 'shaking like a leaf' but she told herself "Give your life, die, but go for it". Her tiny feet danced down the track using all the skills she had practised. She raced ahead to win the gold. She achieved the same distinction in the 800m event. She is now dreaming of the Olympics. With determination and grit she may well achieve her ambition.

Help to Understand

a. All the As complete column A and the Bs complete column B

	A Dinko	B Jyotirmoyee
age		
birth place		
early childhood		
brothers/sisters		
schooling		
sport (skill)		
coach		
awards		

Now the As ask the Bs for details about Jyotirmoyee and fill in column B. Then the Bs ask details about Dinko and fill in column A. Ask questions like "How old is he / she?" "Where was he / she born?"

b. Answer the following questions in a sentence or two:

1. Why did Dinko stay in an orphanage?
2. What gave him some hope in the orphanage?
3. Mention two qualities that helped Dinko survive in difficult conditions?
4. How did Ibonicha help Dinko?
5. What was similar in Dinko's and Jyotirmoyee's childhood years?
6. Jyoti had a slightly different upbringing from that of Dinko – what were the differences?
7. How did her father support her?
8. Why didn't her mother encourage her?
9. When and where did they achieve their ambitions?
10. From your reading of the texts write what are the qualities of a winner?

Useful Words

a. Find the opposites of the following words in the passage. Choose them from the box below:

pleasant	luxury	easy	past	behind
mourned	discourage	hearty	punished	proud

encourage	frugal	miserable	future	difficult
rejoiced	poverty	ahead	humble	rewarded

b. In the previous exercise, the opposite of 'encourage' is 'discourage'. The prefix 'dis' gives a meaning that is opposite of the root word. However prefixes can also be used to mean various things, for example:

Prefix	Meaning	Examples
Auto	Of / by oneself	autograph, auto-pilot , autobiography
Multi	Many	multipurpose, multilingual, multiracial, multinational
Post	After	postwar, postlunch, postgraduate, postdated
Pro	In favour of	pro-government, pro-Indian
Re	Again or back	retype, reread, replace, rewrite
Semi	Half	semifinal, semicircular
Sub	Under	subway, subdivision
Under	Not enough	underworked, undernourished, underpaid

c. Use the table to construct words or phrases to replace the underlined words in the sentences below. You may have to rewrite the sentences:

Example : He is in favour of the American approach.
He is pro-American.

1. Most people say they have to work too hard but are paid too little.
2. He issued a cheque with a date that was later than a real date.
3. He made so many mistakes in the letter that he had to write it again.
4. He works for a company which has branches in many countries.
5. The famous politician decided to write his own story.

Language in Use

Look at the following dialogues:

Sometimes dialogues have words used in spoken English to make the speech seem more natural.

Some of these expressions are – right, okay (your teacher may use these expressions), now, so, good, well then, now then, fine, great, listen, look, I mean, you see, you know, anyway, actually.

Here are some short dialogues. Add some of the expressions given above to make the speech more natural:

Try to use these expressions when you speak to your friends/family/ teachers in a natural way.

Before You Write

a. Here is an excerpt from an interview with Kapil Dev, the famous Indian cricketer. Read the item:

Q : Did you like school?

KD : Well, I liked to play, I never did like school.

Q : Do you owe a lot to your parents and family?

KD : Definitely, everything. They supported me through out.

Q : What has been your training schedule which has kept you so fit?

KD : We have been playing so many matches throughout the year.....

Target ⇒ March'91

b. Work in pairs A and B. A is a junior reporter from a children's magazine called Sunshine. B is the sports champion of Happy Valley School. A is interviewing B for an article in the magazine. Ask and answer questions as given in the example :

A	B
Congratulations! You must be proud of your achievement.	Thank you, yes I am very happy.
What were the events in which you stood first?	Well, I won the 100m, 200m, the javelin throw, long jump, and the pole vault.
That is a big list! How did you practise for these events ?	I used to come to school early in the morning and stay back after school hours to practise.
Who coached you?	Our physical instructor guided me and gave me useful tips.

c. Continue working in pairs. Make a list of five questions and answers. Relate them to any sport, example, basketball, tennis, swimming. Begin your questions with how, what, when, where, who, did, are, and any other words you can think of. Have a variety of questions. Think of interesting answers:

Example : How did you get interested in swimming?

Answer : Well, it is an interesting story. I was just five and quite scared of water. A cousin pushed me into the river flowing near our house and I managed to stay afloat. I enjoyed the experience.

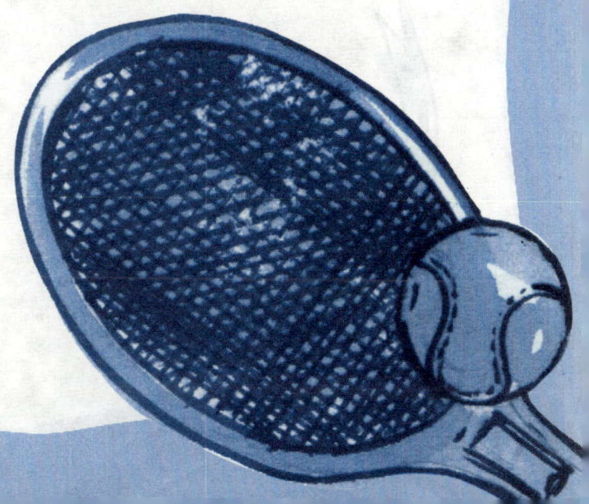

d. Relate the questions to the past, present and the future:

Example:

Q : When did you begin playing tennis? (past)
Ans : I began ....

Q : What is your schedule for practice? (present)
Ans : I normally ....

Q : What do you think you will be doing in ten years time? (future)
Ans : I may/will be ....

e. Share your questions and answers with the rest of the class. Suggest improvements/alterations. Your teacher will write a list of your questions on the blackboard.

Now Write

Using the questions in the list write out an interview between a sports writer and Dinko or Jyotirmoyee. Refer to the text for the answers. Make the answers sound natural. Refer to the section Language in Use, for help in writing.

Game Time

Lost Letter

Change one letter in the top word to get to the second word. Then change one letter in the second word to get to the next and so on till you get to the bottom word:

Example :

S	I	N	G
S	I	N	S
S	O	N	S
T	O	N	S
T	O	N	E
T	U	N	E

1

M	E	N	D
W	A	L	L

2

R	E	A	D
M	E	E	T

5 WOES OF THE WILD

Think : A

What part of the animals is used to make the following items?

Because of man's greed and selfishness these animals have to give up their lives. There are several animals which may disappear from the earth if man does not stop killing them.

Read

The Song of the Whale

Heaving mountain in the sea,
Whale, I heard you
Grieving,
Great Whale, crying for your life,
Crying for your kind, I knew
How we would use
Your dying;

Lipstick for our painted faces,
Polish for our shoes.

Tumbling mountain in the sea,
Whale, I heard you
Calling.
Bird high notes, keening, soaring;
At their edge a tiny drum
Like a heart beat.

We would make you
Dumb.

In the forest of the sea,
Whale, I heard you
Singing.
Singing to your own kind,
We'll never let you be.
Instead of life we choose

Lipstick for our painted faces,
Polish for our shoes.

– Kit Wright

Help to Understand

a. 1. Who is the poet addressing in the poem?

2. What products do we get from a dead whale?

3. The poet is protesting against something—what do you think it is?

4. Pick out the words from the poem that describe the sounds made by the whale. Example: calling .....

5. Why is the whale being compared to a mountain? From the poem pick out the words that describe the "mountain"?

b. In the poem the sea is being compared to a forest in the line "the forest of the sea".

What do you think the following sentences/phrases refer to:

1. The teacher gave a frosty stare when the latecomer walked in.

2. The river Brahmaputra is the sorrow of the East.

3. The Taj Mahal is the jewel of India.

4. Sachin Tendulkar is the pride of the nation.

Think : B

a. Match the following animals with their young ones:

Animals	Young ones
cats	foals
dogs	kittens
horses	calves
sheep	cubs
cows	ducklings
lions	chicken
hens	puppies
ducks	lambs

b. In pairs, discuss the qualities of the young ones:

for example: Babies are helpless. They are tiny and adorable.

How would you describe a little puppy or kitten? Write down some descriptions.

Read

Growing up in the Arctic

Picture a place so cold that oceans freeze, a place where tall trees can't grow, a place where the sun never shines in winter nor sets in summer. There is such a place – it is called the Arctic. It is the world of snow and ice at the North Pole. Polar bears live there.

They are sometimes called ice bears. Nature has given them the things they need to live and be comfortable in the cold weather. They have warm white coats. The hairs of their fur are hollow to trap heat. They store a thick layer of fat under their skin to keep out the cold. Polar bear cubs are usually born in December, in pairs. At birth, they are smaller than a human baby. They are only a foot long and weigh a little more than one pound. Fine white hair covers their bodies. Their eyes are closed and like human babies they can do nothing for themselves.

But polar bear cubs grow quickly. Their mothers feed them on rich milk. Each day they gain weight, their fur grows out and becomes thick. In a couple of weeks their eyes open. After two months they learn to walk. They begin to explore their den and learn how it looks and smells.

By March, the male cub weighs thirty pounds and his sister weighs twenty five pounds. It is time for them to leave the den and learn about the outside world. The cubs are bewildered at first. They have never seen the sky or felt the wind. Each day the cubs are taken outside.

As the days pass the cubs grow stronger and wiser. They learn how to walk in the snow. At first they slip and slide, fall and tumble. But their big square paws help them stay on top of the snow's crust. Their claws grow out and help them grip the surface. The cubs learn by imitating their mother. They growl when their mother growls. When she chases the fox, they follow. When she goes for a walk, the cubs put their feet in her tracks. When she lifts her nose to smell the air, they sniff too. They learn that every animal has its own scent. Their keen noses warn them when danger approaches.

The cubs play in the snow. They run and chase and wrestle with each other. Exercise makes them hungry. The mother nurses them and they grow fat on her milk. When she feels hungry she sets out over fields of snow to catch seals. The cubs follow her putting their paws in her tracks. When they grow tired, they complain with little whines. She stops and lets them nurse. Then she walks faster. The cubs trot behind. After a while they set off for the seashore where the ice is broken and jagged. It is uneven and slippery. The mother moves slowly. The bears have hair on the bottom of their feet and the pads of their toes have tiny cups in the skin. These help them walk without slipping. When she smells the scent of seals she waits patiently and quietly. Seals have good ears. If they hear a bear coming they swim away to safety. A bear will sometimes have to wait for many hours by a breathing hole (hole in the ice used by seals to come up for air) for the seal to return. When it comes back, the bear must move quickly to catch it before it can escape. Eventually, a seal comes to the surface to breathe. The mother bear pounces and drags it out into the ice. She calls her cubs to come and look at the dead seal and taste its meat.

As the months pass, the cubs continue to grow bigger and stronger. After a year they know how to catch seals, but they still have much to learn. They sleep and play and explore new things. At the same time they practice the skills they need when they grow up and have to look after themselves.

By the time they are two years old, they can live alone in the Arctic. They know how to walk over snow and ice and swim in the cold water. They know how to make a bed in the snow and keep warm during the winter storms and they have learned the ways of seals and how to hunt for them. They know how to wash after eating and keep themselves clean. It is time for them to leave their home and go their separate ways.

Help to Understand

a. Complete the following details about polar cubs at birth. Show it to your partner and check if you have got them correctly. Then write the changes that have come about after 3 months.

Polar bear cub (at birth)	After three months
height :	
weight :	
skin/fur :	
activity/movements :	

b. Answer the following questions briefly:

1. Mention four things peculiar to the Arctic region.
2. How has nature helped polar bears to live comfortably in the Arctic region?
3. Why are the cubs bewildered when they see the outside world for the first time?
4. What helps the cubs to walk steadily and firmly?
5. How do the cubs learn to do new things?

6. How does the polar bear catch a seal?

7. What are the skills that the cubs need to know before they can set off on their own?

Useful Words

a. Find synonyms (words that are similar in meaning) for the following words from the text. Check with your partner after completing the exercise:

	Words from the text	synonyms
1.	empty	
2.	cave	
3.	confused	
4.	copying	
5.	feeds	

b. Look at the following combination of verbs from the text:

<u>slip</u> and <u>slide</u>, <u>fall</u> and <u>tumble</u>

They denote two actions that follow one after another. Work with a partner and write out five more combinations. Make them as interesting as possible:

1. ______________________________

2. ______________________________

3. ______________________________

4. ______________________________

5. ______________________________

Language in Use

Look at the following notices:

Feeding
the
animals
is
strictly
prohibited

The above notice means "You are not allowed to feed the animals".

Admission
to
ticket
holders
only

Here it means "Only people with tickets will be allowed to go in".

'Translate' the following notices into everyday English :

Cycles for hire or sale

____

Kindly refrain from smoking in the hall

____

Reduce speed now

____

Penalty for dropping litter-Rs 50

____

Flats to let

Before You Write

In pairs, draw up a list of words that you would use to describe an animal of your choice.

For example: dog: long-eared – Cocker Spaniel
black shiny coat
sad eyes.

Now think of some identifying marks.

Example: a small fold / patch on left hind leg

Now Write

Continue working in pairs. Write a notice for the 'Missing' notice board, describing a pet animal missing from your home. Remember to write the name of the animal, a clear description and the day, time and place when the animal was lost. Mention a reward for the finder. Don't forget to give your contact address.

MISSING

A pet dog, Dodo,

was last seen at ____________________________

on ____________________________

(description) ____________________________

(identifying marks) ____________________________

(reward) ____________________________

(contact address) ____________________________

Game Time

Shelling 'P's

The object of this game is to see who can add the greatest number of 'P's to the following words....

it	ace
at	toe
to	ire
as	la

to change them from one correct word to another. Every 'p' in the word carries one point.

Example : It
Pit - 1 point }
Tip- 1 point } = 2 points.

Now work with the other words. You can score upto 25 points, if you make words with 'p' out of these eight little words.

6 HUMAN FANCIES

Think : A

Work in groups of four. List some latest trends in fashion – in clothes, in hairstyles, in food and others.
Example: clothes – parallels, jeans

Read

Straight Talk

A curly-haired guy who had a passion
For hair styled in the latest fashion,
Wanted to have it standing on end
Without a curl or even a bend.

He tried hair gels, creams and lotions,
Voodoo, hypnosis and magic potions,
He doused his hair in special oil,
Sure to straighten each curl.

But his hair was stubborn – still it curled,
And plain refused to get unfurled.
He listened to tales, macabre and gory,
Hoping it might be a 'hair-raising' story.

But no shock, even an electric one,
Could make his tight curls come undone.
He thought, when brains don't work, of course
You have to rely on plain brute force.

One night he tied each strand with thread
Upto the ceiling above his head,
And dreamed that now his curly tangle,
Would grow along a ninety degree angle.

When he woke up his head felt light –
Had his curls at last given up the fight?
His hand reached up to feel his hair –
But, curly or straight – it wasn't there!

– Vatsala Kaul

macabre	= horrible	doused	= drenched
gory	= unpleasant	voodoo	= black magic

Help to Understand

a. Answer the following questions:

1. Why didn't the man like curly hair?

2. Make a list of the things he used to straighten his hair.

3. How did he try to solve his problem?

4. What happened to his hair?

b. Look at the following phrase.

a <u>curly-haired</u> guy

The underlined word is an adjective describing the man.

The following list of adjectives is from the poem.
Match them with the words they describe in the poem.

latest, curly, electric, macabre, special, hair-raising, tight, gory

Think : B

Read the following conversation:

Ajay : If someone cheats me or steals something from me I won't forgive that person ....

Kavita : I'll repay him or her in the same way.

Abhas : I won't ever talk to that person.

Rakhee : I'll try to find out why he/she did that and then help him/her.

A group of students are talking about an incident that occurred in their classroom. Roshan had tried to steal Monica's bright new pen but had been caught red-handed by his classmates. The teacher has asked the class council to decide on the action to be taken. In groups of four discuss what could be done to solve the problem.

One of you (in your group) could jot down the suggestions:

1. Reasons for Roshan's act ______________________

____

2. Punishment? ______________________

____

3. Forgive and forget? ______________________

____

4. Resolve to behave better. ______________________

____

Your teacher will ask for your suggestions after you have discussed the matter.

Read

The Blue Umbrella

Binya a mountain girl, looked after the cows. One day a group of holiday makers from the city met her and were attracted by the tiger claw charm she wore around her neck. When they offered to buy it from her she wanted the bright blue umbrella in exchange for it. They agreed and Binya was the proud owner of the pretty umbrella. Binya and her umbrella became a common sight. However, Ram Bharosa the tea-stall owner wanted the umbrella very badly. Binya refused to sell it to him. He tried to steal it but proved unsuccessful.

That October every one seemed contented – everyone, that is, except Ram Bharosa.

The old man had by now given up all hopes of ever possessing Binya's umbrella. He wished he had never set eyes on it. Because of the umbrella he had suffered the tortures of greed, the despair of loneliness. Because of the umbrella, people had stopped coming to his shop!

Ever since it had become known that Ram Bharosa had tried to steal the umbrella village people had turned against him. They stopped trusting the old man. Instead of buying their soap and tea and matches from his shop, they preferred to walk an extra mile to the shops at the Tehri bus stand.

The old man sat alone in his empty shop, listening to the eternal hissing of his kettle, and wondering if anyone would ever again step in for a glass of tea. Ram Bharosa had lost his own appetite and ate and drank very little. There was no money coming in. To save money, he had dismissed the blundering Rajaram. So he was left without any company. The roof leaked, and the wind got in through the corrugated tin sheets but Ram Bharosa didn't care.

Bijju and Binya passed his shop almost every day. Bijju went by with a loud but tuneless whistle. But strangely enough, Binya crept quietly past the shop, looking the other way, almost as though she was in some way responsible for the misery of Ram Bharosa.

She kept reasoning with herself, telling herself that the umbrella was her very own, and that she couldn't help it if others were jealous of it. But had she loved the umbrella too much? Had it mattered more to her than people mattered? She couldn't help feeling that in a small way she was the cause of the sad look on Ram Bharosa's face. The ruinous condition of his shop was all due to his own greed, no doubt; but she didn't want him to feel too bad about what he'd done, because it made her feel bad about herself; and so she closed the umbrella whenever she came near the shop, opening it again only when she was out of sight.

One day towards the end of October, when she had ten paise in her pocket, she entered the shop and asked the old man for a toffee.

She was Ram Bharosa's first customer in almost two weeks. He looked suspiciously at the girl. Had she come to taunt him, to flaunt the umbrella in his face? She had placed her coin on the counter. Perhaps it was a bad coin. Ram Bharosa picked it up and bit it, he held it up to the light, he rang it on the ground. It was a good coin. He gave Binya the toffee.

Binya had already left the shop when Ram Bharosa saw the closed umbrella lying on his counter. There it was, the blue umbrella he had always wanted, within his grasp at last! He had only to hide it at the back of his shop, and no one would know that he had it, no one could prove that Binya had left it behind.

"But I'm never in the sun or in the rain," he said aloud. "Of what use is an umbrella to me?"

And he hurried outside and ran after Binya. "Binya, Binya!" he shouted. "Binya, you've left your umbrella behind!"

He wasn't used to running, but he caught up with her, held out the umbrella, saying, "You forgot it - the umbrella!"

In that moment it belonged to both of them. But Binya didn't take the umbrella. She shook her head and said, "You keep it. I don't need it any more."

"But it's such a pretty umbrella!" protested Ram Bharosa. "It's the best umbrella in the village."

"I know," said Binya. "But an umbrella isn't everything."

And she left the old man holding the umbrella, and went tripping down the road, and there was nothing between her and the bright blue sky.

– **Ruskin Bond**

Help to Understand

a. Given below is a summary of the story. But the sentences are mixed up. Put them in the correct order. Work in pairs:

1. As there was no money coming in, he had to dip into his savings.
2. He was unhappy because he wanted to possess the blue umbrella at all cost.
3. When Binya saw the lonely old man she felt she was responsible for his sadness.
4. Added to this, he had no one to talk to.
5. It was the pleasant month of October and everyone, except Ram Bharosa, seemed happy.
6. So, when he tried to steal it, the villagers stopped coming to his shop.
7. Although Ram Bharosa was tempted to take it he ran after Binya and returned it.
8. She said that an umbrella wasn't everything and went away happily.
9. But Binya didn't take it.
10. One day she went to his shop and asked for a toffee.

Now rewrite the sentences in the correct order.

For example, sentence no.5 is the first sentence of the story :
It was the pleasant month of October and everyone, except Ram Bharosa, seemed happy.

b. Answer the following questions in a sentence or two:

1. Why was Ram Bharosa unhappy?
2. Why didn't the villagers trust Ram Bharosa?
3. How did they show this distrust?
4. Why did Binya feel guilty when she passed his shop?
5. What did Binya do to comfort Ram Bharosa?
6. Why did Ram Bharosa run after Binya with the umbrella?
7. What makes you feel that Binya was happy after she had given away the umbrella?

Useful Words

a. Idioms are words that describe people, places, things, feelings, moods and situations using qualities associated with other objects.

Example : She has a <u>heart of gold</u> = very kind, generous.
He's rather a <u>cold fish</u> = unfriendly

1. In pairs read the story again and pick out idioms associated with qualities, moods, objects.

Example:
The sunlight was mellow = soft, soothing.

2. Now divide them into two columns positive and negative. Write them in the appropriate columns.

If they are neither, put them in the neutral column:

Positive	Negative	Neutral
Example: kind (month)		

b. Try to make up 5 idioms about any two of the following:

people, objects, feelings, moods.

Show them to your partner.

Your teacher will ask you to read out the idioms.

Language in Use

Here is a piece of the dialogue between Ram Bharosa and Binya when she went to his shop:

Binya : Could I have some toffee, please?

Ram Bharosa : Well, how many do you want?

Binya : ..... I have ten paise.. and I was wondering how many ......

Ram Bharosa : That's two toffees and no change.

Binya : Thank you, that will do fine.

Ram Bharosa : You're welcome, here are your toffees.

In pairs make up a similar dialogue between a bookseller and a student. The following expressions may be useful:

Could you / I

I wonder

I'm afraid we don't have

You may / might

It could ...

That's all right.

Before You Write

A group of villagers decide to form a committee to draw up certain rules of conduct for themselves in order to prevent unpleasantness and misunderstanding in the community.

Form groups of four. Write down five or six rules of conduct:

For example: We must help those who are in trouble.

Now Write

Make up a poster to be put up in the village square in the space given below.

Game Time

Brain Teaser

Every year, a garage presents its thousandth visitor with a free car stereo. Four cars have come to the garage. The fourth one is the thousandth car. Here is some work for your brains. Look at the number plates and find the lucky winner.

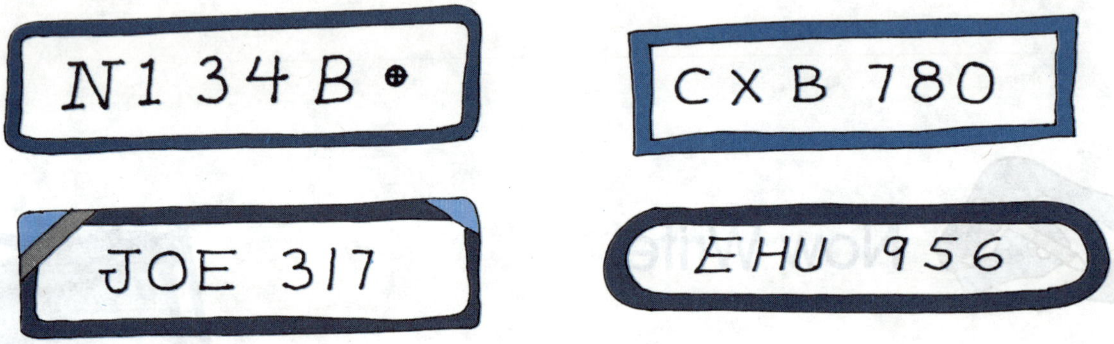

The numberplate of the first car has two of the first four letters of the alphabet.

The numberplate of the second car has a Christian name.

The numberplate of the third car has numbers which add up to more than 18.

Who is the happy owner of the thousandth car?

7 PERFORMING ACTS

Think : A

Name some acts that are performed on stage, in front of an audience.

Read the poem given below. It describes how an empty plastic bag is tossed around by the wind. The bag seems to perform a ballet dance.

Read

The Performing Bag

The plastic bag that once was full
Of coloured sweets, was empty and lost,
And lay against the playground wall,
Flat and still among the dust.

But a wind came up the road,
Brushing back the hair of the grass,
Trying to unbutton people's coats,
And teasing the leaves as it passed.

It felt its way inside the bag,
Like a hand inside a glove.
And like a puppet waking up
The plastic bag began to move.

As the air inside it puffed it out,
The bag that was lying sad and flat,
Began to waggle its corners about,
And nodded its head this way and that.

It dodged its way between the children,
Who watched it carried high in the sky,
And disappear on the hand of the wind,
Waving them goodbye

– **Stanley Cook**

Help to Understand

a. Answer the following questions:

1. What was inside the plastic bag before it became empty?
2. What did the wind do to the grass, people's coats and the leaves? What is the wind being compared to?
3. What happened to the bag when the wind found its way inside it?
4. What did the children do?
5. How and where did the bag disappear?

b. It felt its way inside the bag
"Like a hand inside a glove"

'It' refers to the 'wind'.
The wind is being compared to
a hand and the bag to a glove.

Such comparisons are called similes. Find another example of a simile in the poem.

Here are some commonly used similes:

as bold as brass,
as white as snow / a sheet
as quick as a flash
as deaf as a post
as blind as a bat
as mad as a hatter
as quiet as a mouse
as hard as nails

c. Complete the following sentences by selecting suitable similes:

1. Asha is ____________ as ____________ as you wouldn't believe the crazy things she does.

2. He never says anything. He is as ____________ as ____________

3. I'm afraid I can't read this small print. I'm as ____________ as ____________

4. She was very clever. The answer came to her as ____________ as ____________

5. When he saw the ghost, his face went as ____________ as ____________

Think : B

a. Work in pairs:

Rearrange the following letters to make a word which means "a robot copy of a man or a woman"

n o i r a d d

If you don't know the answer look at the next page.

b. If you had a machine that could do a lot of work for you, think of the things it could help you with at home and at school.

Example: dusting

Make a list of ten such things. Compare your list with that of others in the class.

Read

Robots – Fact and Fiction

What is a robot?

Quite simply, a robot is a machine that is capable of independent action. In other words, it must be able to perform a given task without being continually supervised by man. In contrast, a remote-controlled machine needs someone to control its every movement. Yet many people often confuse the two types of machines.

To illustrate the important difference it is worth looking at a remote-controlled device called the 'Wheelbarrow'. It is used by the army and police forces to inspect cars that are suspected of containing a bomb. The operator is able to sit well back in safety and direct the machine to the car by means of a radio or cable link. Wheelbarrow carries a television camera which allows the operator to see exactly what is happening. He can then manipulate Wheelbarrow's mechanical arm to smash the car window to look inside.

If the Wheelbarrow were a robot rather than a remote controlled machine, events would be quite different. The robot would approach the car independently, check underneath, open the doors and then locate the explosive device (if there was one). It may even be able to diffuse the bomb without any additional commands.

However, in order to be a robot, the Wheelbarrow would need two very important features. First, it would need a brain—a computer that would store and operate and give instructions that a robot needs as to how to go about doing a particular job. Secondly, for it to act independently it would need to be able to gather and analyze all sorts of information about its immediate surroundings and the job it is working on - a process known as feedback.

It is these two features – the brain and some form of feedback – that allow a robot to be a truly independent machine, capable of doing a number of different tasks.

Robots today are in the second stage of their development and these stages are referred to as 'generations'. First-generation robots are quite basic machines. They have a simple brain and are good at doing exactly what they are told to do. However, they have no feedback - no sensing ability to tell them that something is wrong and what they should do about it.

(Answer: Android)

The robots used in car factories to weld body panels and spray the car shells, for example, would continue to operate even though a fault on the assembly line had delayed the components.

However, robot engineers are now working to perfect the next generation of machines. In contrast, these second generation robots will have many human-like senses. They will be able to see, if only in a limited way, and they will also be able to feel. So they will be able to tell whether there is a car shell in front of them or not. Sophisticated manipulators (arms) will give these robots the ability to 'feel' the shape and texture of an object.

It is also quite likely that the new machines will be able to speak, rather than having to communicate by printer or visual display unit as at present.

Help to Understand

a. Say whether the following statements are true or false:

1. A robot can act on its own.
2. The 'Wheelbarrow' can act independently.
3. A robot has a brain.
4. Robots in car factories stop working when something goes wrong.
5. Second generation robots will be able to speak.

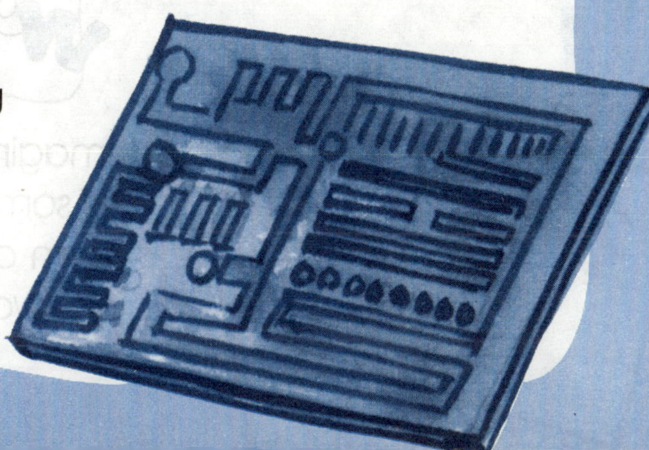

b. Here are some phrases that describe a robot and a remote-controlled machine. Write the phrases in the respective columns under Robot / Remote Controlled Machine:

⇒ Capable of independent action

⇒ Has a brain

⇒ Can do a variety of jobs

⇒ Can do a job as directed by the operator

⇒ It has a TV camera that allows the operator to see the actor

⇒ Can gather and analyse information about the job it is working on

⇒ Someone controls its movements

Robot	Remote-Controlled Machine

c. What are the differences between first and second generation robots?

Useful Words

a. Imagination means 'to form mental images of something that is not present'. It is the noun form of the verb 'imagine'. Here are some 'tion' words. Give the root forms of these words:

noun	verb
inspection	________
operation	________
direction	________
manipulation	________
location	________
instruction	________
information	________
communication	________

b. Complete the following sentences with the correct form of the verbs given above :

1. Ram was a stranger in town. He did not know where the bank was ________
2. The classrooms were clean and tidy as the supervisor was due any moment to ________ them.
3. The manager asked his secretary to ________ the officers that the meeting had been postponed.
4. The machine had grown rusty. He could not ________ it although he tried to move it in all directions.
5. He did not know French, so he could not ________ effectively to the audience in Paris.

Language in Use

a. Look at the following expressions from the text you have just read and in pairs discuss why such expressions are used.

so much so
quite simply
in other words,
in contrast
to illustrate the ....
for example
however,
so,
first
secondly.

The reasons may be
- to organise a piece of writing
- to explain something
- to rephrase something
- to emphasise

Arrange the phrases given above under the following headings:

Organisation	Explanation	Emphasis Memorising	Rephrasing
first	for example	so much so	in other words

Add two more words/phrases to each category.

b. Complete the following piece of writing using some of the expressions given above :

In ancient times nobody needed money because everybody worked together and shared things. In bigger societies people have skills. One person spends all his time making pots and another spends all his time fishing.The fisherman needs pots and the potter needs fish, which they exchange or barter.

________________ this system can became very complicated if, ________________ the potter wants ten fish but the fisherman wants only one pot. ________________ people began to use money.

Before You Write

1. Read the following descriptions :

"Emma Wodehouse, beautiful, clever and rich seemed to have some of the best blessings of life......."

"Grandmother was always dressed in white. She had snow white hair and her face had a thousand wrinkles....."

Work in pairs. List all the describing words from the above descriptions.

____

____

2. Think of a person – a cousin, an uncle, aunt, grandparent, a parent. First write three sentences to describe the physical appearance of the person.
Example: tall, short, plump, slim, fair, dark (complexion).

____

____

Next write three sentences to describe the qualities.
Example: friendly, shy, intelligent, kind.

____

____

____

Now, think of your feelings towards the person. Example: I like ... . He / she enjoys my company ... . Write two sentences. Now you have a complete description of the person.

Now Write

Write a description of your favourite person in paragraphs. Give a title.

Example: My Favourite Aunt, My Best Friend

Follow the three examples in the Before You Write section.

Game Time

Think of ten different ways in which an ordinary object could be used.

Example: an empty coke can

Uses – flower vase, pen stand, paperweight, candle stand, soap dish, drum, measuring can, watering can, stool...

8 BOBBY

Think

What would you do to make a history lesson interesting?

In pairs, jot down two or three suggestions.

Discuss these with the other students and your teacher.

Read

Bobby

Scene I

[Bobby is sitting alone in her room, the sun has not yet set, but it's fast approaching twilight]

Bobby : It's so boring, sitting here all alone, makes me sound like the proverbial Jack, "all work and no play" and a "dull" girl. And remembering these history dates are so difficult. Why should I read in which year Akbar fought some battle or when Shivaji killed Afzalkhan? Can't they make these history lessons more interesting? I am sure Akbar and Shivaji never thought of the problems they were creating for us. Oh, for some fun...

[Akbar is seated on his throne, with a worried look on his face. Enter Birbal, thought to be the wisest man in Akbar's court]

Birbal : Goood moornning, Emperor Akbar [in the same intonation of a class saying "good morning" to its teacher]. Emperor, you look very pensive. What is the problem?

Akbar : I have been ruling since the age of thirteen, but have never faced such a peculiar situation. Birbal, the students of the kingdom are rebelling, and I don't know what can be done? At least with Hemu and other kings, I could wage a battle and defeat them at war, but how do I deal with this lot? I cannot declare war against children.

Birbal : That's indeed a grave situation, Emperor. What are their demands?

Akbar : They are revolting against the education syllabus which they say places more emphasis on memory rather than allowing them to be creative. They say that History is riddled with dates and battle-grounds, English is full of formal sentence constructions and pronunciations which have no relation to the spelling, and Mathematics is far too complex for their age.

Birbal : I must admit Emperor, that their demands seem justified. But are they willing to negotiate? Who is their leader?

Akbar : A girl called Bobby is leading the group, and she seems adamant.

Birbal : I think we should call for a Round Table Conference and discuss these issues with her.

Scene II

[Bobby addressing a group of students who clap after every sentence of hers].

Bobby : ...and we are determined that till our demands are met, we will not give an inch. [claps] "Swaraj is our birthright and we shall have it." [claps] We want a better syllabus and more interesting periods. [loud claps with shouts of "Bobby zindabad"]

[Enter Messenger I, in a hurried state]

Messenger I : Leader, leader [in a whisper to Bobby], I just heard the news that they are planning to assassinate you, just like the way it happened with Abraham Lincoln. We feel that you should go underground.

Bobby : [The news disturbs her, but there is no change in her face]. We shall fight to the last, and I ask you students to support this great cause. "Ask not what your country can do for you, but what you can do for your country..."

[Enter Messenger II from Emperor Akbar's court, carrying a pamphlet, which he opens and reads out]

Messenger II : [in the tone of a proclamation, of one reading out a notice]. For whomsoever it may concern. It has been brought to the notice of the *Jahanpanah** Akbar that some rebellious activity is taking place in the kingdom of the Emperor. The Emperor, being just and kind, has issued this notice calling for a Round Table Conference. All those who have any grievances can attend this Conference. A special invitation is extended to Bobby, supposedly the leader of the rebellion.... The Conference will also mark the tenth anniversary celebration of the Emperor's win over Hemu at the second battle of Panipat in 1557...

Bobby : [suspiciously] There might be a plot here to assassinate me. But, I shall definitely go. [addressing her followers]. Bring in the horses, and let us gallop into the night and reach the court early.

* *Jahanpanah - Title given to Emperors*

Scene III

Shivaji : [thinking to himself]. That's definitely a plot to kill Bobby. Haven't I faced a similar situation? Didn't Aurangzeb try to kill me when he had called me to his court. But of course, he stood no chance against my foresight. I was too clever for him. I escaped in a fruit basket. I think I will present Bobby with the same fruit basket, just in case she also requires it. And I will make it a point to be present at the Round Table Conference for Bobby might require my help.

Scene IV

Bobby : [at home] It's growing dark, and mama and papa have not returned. I have been a "good girl" – finished my homework, had my dinner, and am ready to sleep – what's taking them so long?

[A mouse scurries by]

Bobby : Ha, Mickey Mouse, what are you doing here, roaming around stealthily in the night?

Mickey Mouse : [in a sad tone and with an American accent]. What's me to do, Bo-bhay? It's all these wars. Bosina, Middle East, Sudan, Libya, Afghanistan. So, there's a shortage of food everywhere. Even India is at war, but I keep hearing your Miss World, Ashwaaryaa Raai, say India's the land of peace and non-violence, so I shifted here looking for some food and peace of mind. But, man, it was real tough, reaching here. I sailed as a stowaway on Columbus' ship and reached West Indies. From there, I managed to hitch- hike with Vasco-da-Gama. Somehow I reached Calcutta. The food on these ships was really bad, I hardly got to nibble on anything, but Calcutta is real fun especially on the Metro Railway and the trams.

Bobby : Oh, you poor soul, let me get you something. [opens the fridge and gives Mickey Mouse some bread crumbs]. [A content Mickey Mouse gulps them down hungrily].

Mickey Mouse : [with a tear in the eye] Thank you so very much, Bo-bhay. I knew I would find some peace and care in India [goes away humming the song, "I love my India"].

Bobby : [thinking aloud] What's this world come to, with all the fights and battles? But I have problems of my own...It's getting dark, and I am getting scared...My parents haven't returned yet. Maybe, if I move the clock ahead, they will appear.

[Bobby moves the hands of the clock to 12. There's a loud clang as the clock strikes. An eerie darkness envelopes the room and Bobby lets out a frightened shriek.]

Bobby : What's this? How did it get dark so soon?

A Voice : Because it is night by the clock.

Bobby : [looking around] Who's that?

A Voice : It's me. Your friendly neighbourhood moon.

Bobby : Ah! The soothing, charming moon. I have read a lot about your beauty.

Moon : So, why don't you look at me more often? You know, I feel sad, when you look at me only when you are lonely and tired. Sometimes, I do want you to look at me when you are smiling. That way, when I am tired, I will feel relaxed. Everybody nowadays only pays attention to the sun, but I had my revenge on him recently when I eclipsed him.

Bobby : Oh! I never thought of it that way. That's true. Okay, I promise I will look at you every night

without fail. And when you are in your full bloom, I will plant a huge smile on my face, and when you disappear for a night, I will wait longingly for you to come back.

Moon : [to herself] That's my Bobby. Always kind and considerate. Yet sad, for who's to make her happy? I will take up her issue at the Round Table Conference.

Scene V

[The scene of the Round Table Conference. The chairs are arranged in a circular fashion with an elevated throne at the centre for the presiding officer. There are many who have come to witness the conference. These include children of varying age groups, some parents and general public. They are seated in two rows behind the seats for the round table conference.]

[Everybody rises as Emperor Akbar, dressed in his ceremonial attire, enters and seats himself on the throne. Shivaji, invisible to everyone else, places himself on an imaginary throne next to Akbar.]

Akbar : Let the proceedings of the Round Table Conference begin. [addressing his secretary]. I hope you are taking down the minutes of the meeting. Ah! Bobby, it's good that you are present. I hear you are leading the rebellion against the state. What are your grievances, my child?

Bobby : [her angry look disappears at the mention of the word 'child']. Jahanpanah, we are displeased with the way we are being taught. The texts are too difficult for our age. We have too many books to read and carry to school. Many students even find it difficult to lift their school-bags. Also, many of the texts are not at all interesting.

[There are loud cheers and claps of the children as Bobby speaks]

Akbar : Silence! This is not a fish market, but a serious conference. Everybody will be given their chance to speak. Birbal, what do you have to say about this? Why are the children of our kingdom burdened with so many books?

Birbal : Emperor, we too do not like to prescribe so many books. But then, how else will they learn so many things? They have to learn all about your achievements in battle and the *nav-ratans* in your court. They have to understand the concepts of the earth, the moon, the sun, work out equations and sums in mathematics. All these require books, Jahanpanah.

Akbar : But is there not a way by which they learn all this, find it interesting and yet have smaller books?

[Mickey Mouse who has been sitting quitely all this while, starts speaking]

Mickey Mouse : Emperor, I have toured this country extensively, on ships and trains and planes and bullock-carts. And I thought it would be a great thing to teach the children about historical figures like me. We have no dates attached to us. We were never born, nor will we ever die. We don't fight any battles. We are full of wit and wisdom and always bring a smile to the lips of every child...

Birbal : [intervening] There has been a similar suggestion from some states that we prepare a Reader for students which provides all the learning material in a simplified and interesting form with lovely illustrations. If we were to follow that then...

Akbar : Why the delay in implementing such a plan? We should immediately issue a notice that from now onwards all learning will be in the form of the Readers prepared specially keeping in mind the needs of the students.

[Shivaji now decides to make himself visible to everyone].

Shivaji : I have been listening to this discussion and think that it's a brilliant idea to have Readers. They will be fun, interesting and more helpful. I shall immediately direct my followers to implement this scheme in my state.

[All the audience clap at this suggestion]

[The moon enters gasping]

Moon : Shivaji Maharaj, Emperor Akbar…wait. Don't dismiss the Conference.

Shivaji and Akbar : What's the matter? Take a seat, relax, have a glass of water.

Moon : Thank you sirs, I came running all the way, since I also wanted to point out that Bobby is very sad.

[An ignorant male voice springs from the audience]

Ignorant Male Voice: That will happen if both parents go to work and leave her alone at home.

Shivaji : Who dares insult working parents?

Akbar : Guards, catch that man, and put him in prison for making such ignorant statements.

[A commotion ensues, as the guards catch the man, known to be a big bully, who mistreats everyone].

Birbal : Oh! The folly of men, to blame everything on parents. Did not Tansen sing a delightful ode, the other day, to the new independent woman, who believes working is her right and yet manages to take care of her children? She lets her children be independent and free, prepares them to face the world without tugging at her apron strings. She does not force her children to "Do this and do that", but rather lets them grow to be themselves.

And above all, Bobby's parents care a great deal for her. Did not her father take leave and take care of Bobby when she was down with Malaria and cook that delightful soup? Did not her mother buy her the computer she wanted and take her out to the cricket match? Yet, Bobby is sad, and there are many children like her, equally sad, and so we must do something for them.

[A slight murmur of agreement goes round the audience, especially among the section of the children]

[There is a general discussion among the conference members. More specifically, Shivaji and Akbar, converse in great detail. After a while the Conference pronounces a resolution]

The members of the Conference are of the unanimous opinion that all states should pronounce under Section 2000 of the Indian Penal Code a law making it compulsory to use Readers to teach students. Furthermore, it is stated that since all the children are sad and want interesting activities, they will be taken to different places each day of the week. On Monday, Shivaji Maharaj will take them to one of his forts, Tuesday, they will be accorded a place among the nav-ratans of Emperor Akbar. On Wednesday, the moon will guide them across the universe, while on Thursday, Mickey Mouse will travel with them to Disneyland. Friday, everyone will have to put in time with Birbal and recount whatever they have learnt the previous days.

[Loud cheers and claps ring through the room. Some students come and lift Bobby on their shoulder and Bobby comes out of the conference room flashing a 'V' sign. The area is surrounded by cameramen and reporters from Doordarshan, Star News, Zee and others, who are giving a live telecast of the conference proceedings to the nation. All of them crowd Bobby, congratulate her and take her photographs. A bearded gentleman often seen on television during election times

tries to push his way through the crowds for an exclusive interview with Bobby.]

Bobby : [at home in bed now and glowing in the limelight]. But what happens on the remaining two days?

[All the characters together]

On the remaining days, you spend time with your lovely parents.

Bobby : Oh! I am so glad and happy. Life will be so full of fun. And it is so selfish of me to be disappointed at Mama and Papa not being there. Here, they come...

[Bobby pretends to be asleep]

Mamma : Bobby dear, sorry we are late today. See, what we have got for you.

Papa : She's asleep. Must have been tired. Let her sleep.

[The lights slowly dim. Bobby sleeps peacefully with a smile on her face while her parents go about their own chores. As the lights dim out totally, Bobby opens one eye and looks at the audience]

Ta-ta, bye-bye, good night and... sweet dreams.

Help to Understand

a. Now that you have read the play, say whether the following statements are true or false:

1. Bobby is a boy.
2. Bobby's is sitting alone at home.
3. Bobby lives in a world of imagination.
4. There is peace all over the world.
5. Bobby is very good at remembering dates.
6. Bobby is the leader of the students.
7. The moon is sad that no one looks at her.
8. Mickey Mouse sailed with Shivaji to Calcutta.
9. Bobby pretends to sleep when her parents come home.
10. Tansen is the wisest person in Akbar's court.

b. Work in pairs. Suggest reasons for the following statements:

Statements	Reason
Example : Bobby doesn't like history.	History is full of dates.
a. Akbar calls for a Round Table Conference.	
b. Mickey Mouse shifted to India.	
c. Mickey is always hungry.	
d. The moon feels sad.	
e. Shivaji attends the Round Table Conference.	
f. The new independent woman goes to work.	
g. Bobby is cheered by everyone after the Conference.	

Tips for play acting:

Divide the class into 3 groups – the first group will be the actors group, the second group will be the costume group and the third the stage preparation group.

The teacher will be the director.

The actors need not learn the dialogues if they are doing it for their class. They can read their parts from his book or repeat after the teacher. However, if they are to stage this play for the school assembly then the actors should learn the dialogue.

For the Love of a Cat continued ...

The next day, the painter worked furiously. As the sun set the last brush-stroke was made. He opened the door to the courtyard. "It is finished," he said.

All next day the priests marvelled at his wonderful painting. The painter sat in the courtyard, tired but satisfied. After many months he now rested.

Suddenly the painter was surrounded by noise and anger. "You scoundrel! You have cheated us!"

"What a thing to do! We interfered with nothing – and yet you deceived us!"

What had he done? "A cat! He put a cat near the feet of the Holy One!" cried one priest. All the priests were furious.

"Tomorrow," said the head priest, "you will be disgraced in front of the whole town. Your painting will be publicly burned, and you will be thrown on the streets. You will never paint again."

The painter was bundled away under guard. The doors were locked on the room where the painting was kept.

At dawn the next morning, the people of the town gathered around the temple to see the painter's shame. He was dragged before them, pale but quiet. He knew what he had done. In a way, the priests were right. But in his heart he knew they were wrong. Still, now it was too late. His life was over. If he was not permitted to paint, he had no wish to live.

Silence fell over the crowd, as the head priest explained what the painter had done. "We told him the Holy One did not like cats. We gave him this one condition only. But he betrayed our trust. He drew a cat at the feet of the Holy One! He has shown disrespect, and must be given the severest punishment. Open the temple doors!" he cried, "Bring out the painting for burning!"

All turned to watch as the great doors were swung open.

Two priests went inside to fetch the painting. As they brought it out into light, the whole crowd gasped. The seated Buddha was smiling, and on his lap with his hand gently resting on it, was the little cat.

"It's a miracle!" went up a cry. And so it was. The priests were humble enough to understand their fault. The painter was given all honour both for his painting, and, when the full story was known, for his great love for one of God's creatures, too.